True Compassion

Merging Love Into Oneness

Saint Germain

11-22-2022

Indeed, that grand Loving potential for Mastering the quality of Lasting True Compassion dwells in-born within your Human heart. With your surrendered alignment and diligent practice, this long overdue quality within Humanity can gracefully thrive and expand in your consciousness, joining with like-minded multitudes throughout the Earth World. Shaped as an energetic Heart-space of pure energy, True Compassion stands ready to synchronously open the portal of Oneness for all Humanity, at long last folding together the auras of man and woman melded in Divine Partnership.

≁ ≁

I call to all Humankind around the Earth World, in these pivotal moments of Human civilization's now undetermined fate, to willingly and consciously instill a permanent and lasting

New Paradigm of Compassion

from this moment forward. The individual and collective consciousness of All Humanity, refined and embraced by the open Portal for this vibration of True Compassion, will position Love to inflow and, at last, merge into
Oneness upon Earth.

The free-will choice is squarely in your hands,
My Dearest Ones of Humankind.

≁ ≁

OVERVIEW

*T*he shining Light of True Compassion dwells within the surrendered Heart-space of every aligned Spiritual Being. As Saint Germain, My intention in this book is to inspire and impart practical Loving Spiritual guidelines for the Hearts of you women and men of Earth, … united together, … to discover, practice, and actually live a *New Paradigm of True Compassion* to thrive and long endure in your own Personal Universes and beyond. Those Ones you then touch with this visceral vibration will also be truly Blessed, as radiating Compassion opens the Portal for Love to shine exponentially and brilliantly into your Earth World.

This book provides a foundation to accomplish this purpose of installing in your consciousness a lasting practice of delivering these Nurturing Elements of True Compassion, Merging Love into Oneness.

Develop and expand your capabilities to make the necessary changes in your belief-system to embrace and allow needed heart openings, non- judgements, Spiritual alignments, boundaries, Being the Giver, wise choices, and forgiveness.

All told, the saving grace for Humanity is Love in action. This Dharmic thread links the inborn abilities of all Humans to deliver True Compassion wrapped in the reality of Oneness.

Maintaining this higher vibration is known to accelerate your progress into the Higher 5th, 7th and 9th Dimensions of Human evolvement.

As you read on, My words will begin to unspool for your ongoing understanding and enlightenment. When you align, True Compassion will be yours, lodged as a full-time resident in your Personal Universe.

*Join with Me now, for the sake of All Human civilization, to bring this **New Paradigm of Compassion** into Being.*

HIGHLAND LIGHT PUBLISHERS ®

Oceanside, CA. 92056-6237

First Edition 2023
Highland Light Publishers

This Work may be ordered
by visiting Amazon.com or
Barns and Noble.
or through independent and chain book sellers, online retailers
worldwide.

The views expressed in this book are conditioned by the Disclaimer
which follows. Certain stock imagery © Dreamstime.com., 123RF.com
and Gordon W .Corwin II.

Saint Germain

Portrait Marius Fine Art

TABLE OF CONTENTS

BOOKS BY THIS AUTHOR

ক্ষ্যক্ষ

THE SAINT GERMAIN CHRONICLES COLLECTION
A Journey Into Practical Spirituality

VICTORY FOR THE SOUL
Relationships That Work

RISING ABOVE
A Journey To Higher Dimensions

ANGER HEALING AND TRANSMUTATION
An Elevation Of The Soul

TRUE GRATITUDE - Quan Yin

An Open Hand Of Love

Higher Dimensions of consciousness await you, My Good Friends … launching from the 3rd Dimension to the 5th, and onward to the 7th and finally arriving at the 9th Dimension, if that be your path.

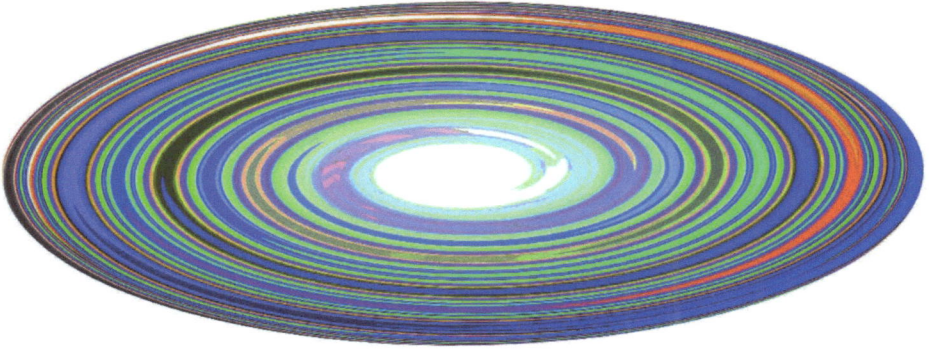

Wisely and brilliantly broadcasting the shining *Light of True Compassion* is the purpose of My writing and speaking this day.

Be heartened that developing and anchoring the following fundamental Elements of True Compassion will profoundly apply to enhancing your progress of overall Spiritual evolvement as well. Perhaps this offers an enticing tidbit for your Ego to step aside?

In a nutshell, … when you successfully *open the Heart-space for creating the energy of the* **New Paradigm of Compassion**, … *you shall need to have* totally wiped out and eliminated your judgements that could surround any portion of the Object person or circumstance at hand. *Then, your viscerally heartful vibration of Oneness may enter the scene, front stage center. The purity and clarity of this resulting space in your consciousness will then have the power to 'gain traction', as you Humans might phrase it.*

Once Humanity finally learns that fear can be transcended by the applied power of Love in Action, the sword can be lain aside, and Oneness shall take its rightful Cosmic Domain upon Earth.

Lacking the above qualities for sourcing Compassion, you yourself risk becoming part of the problem!

Capiche?

Simple as that!

Alright!

Now for the nurturing ingredients needed for you to stir into the mixing pot.

11

*A*s *for all emotions*, **this heartful call for Compassion** deserves its own special attention and tendering before it is acted upon. *The Elements of Compassion, The Process of Delivery, and The Merit of a Circumstance* are all on the list for consideration *in the eyes of the Giver* before delivering the 'Giver's' Gift of free-will choice. Due care and consideration need be applied with a keen awareness, appropriate for gifting this heartful vibration … for you to enter the picture ... directing energy toward *the receiver, the 'Object'* of your Compassion.

When your gift of True Compassion is *heartfully delivered*, you will viscerally know it is wrapped in selfless love, freely outflowing, … without even a glimpse or a hint of *quid pro quo expectations* … getting something in return … save the joy you feel.

These Compassion-giving moments of choice as the Giver may simply *appear* in your life, at times as casual, or with heart wrenching urgency, as some situations may well Be.

And so, at this pivotal juncture for expansion of your Earthly consciousness in motion, lies either a magnificent opportunity to sprinkle Compassion … *where sense of merit-worthiness appears* … into the mix, … **or** to simply withhold delivering an action involving yourself, with no further emotional engagement of Compassion per se in this context, ... with all actions embraced by your *free-will choice, without guilt or obligation.*

As a **'Giver of Compassion'**, you are delivering, <u>within your Human pay grade,</u> … a Blessing to the Object of your Compassion. Are you with me?

> ## *Know this:*
>
> ### *The gracious gift of Loving Compassion sourced from your Earthly Dimensional consciousness is, in the <u>Human version</u>, akin and mildly analogous to the energy released from an Angel's touch sourced from their 10th Dimensional lair.*

Give Me a person in some significant measure of distress (or simply 'overly stressed' as you may label it), follow My instructions, and *you may then effectively apply the guidelines for making your free-will choices about delivering the vibration of Compassion that suits.*

A *Spiritual sense of worthiness* of the situation at hand, along with wise use of your *Giver's boundaries,* … all merit conscious attention, My Fine Feathered Friends, … lest you, on the one hand, be callously *detached* and deliver a shallow superficial gesture, … or beyond this … so foolishly entangled that you yourself are sucked into the maelstrom of the circumstance, with your own emotions and triggers then flaring up and activating you to become entangled as a *co-participant of the circumstance*! If the latter outcome be the case, you will need to unleash a mighty dose of Compassion upon your own foolish self, yes? (Master chuckles gleefully…)

Alright! To continue … we've digressed a bit as I often do in these discourses for you.

Let Us now delve into some greater depth. Your heartful thought or feeling that identifies with the distress of persons and their circumstance can often translate into an engaging onset of emotions of your own, indeed, if you are not careful!

I speak of a visceral vibration that often plucks a heart string or two. And at times, a matching feeling of your own internal pain transference can ride along on the back of these emotions.

And ... you need be aware to recognize that this feeling, engagingly heartful as it may nonetheless be, need not engulf you into the quagmire of the circumstance itself! Read on My Fine Friends.

Remember, as a Dimensional Spiritual Being, ... you are *observing* here, as a potential Compassion Giver, about to make a Free-will choice of consequence, ... as you will soon see.

As this observer, *you are looking from the outside in*, versus as an <u>involved person</u>, tangled in the mix, biting nails and wringing hands, ... *looking from the inside out*.

You are thereby able to also <u>choose</u> your own level of relating to the *Object person and circumstance* ... and nonetheless allowing, ... not blocking, *your own emotions* to freely flow ... <u>AND</u> *without inducing any unnecessary action on your part,* without entangling further thought or deed on your part, ... before, during, and after the Compassion process. In a sense, you now become the <u>detached observer of yourself!</u> Advanced indeed.

19

Once You have reached out and touched the 'Object person … and/or circumstance … with delivery of your heartful energy I speak of, that extension could well *complete this process for you.* FINITO! Boundaries will follow.

Remember, the Object receiver is responsible to handle their/its own circumstance, … with **or** without any attendant emotions they may choose to act upon. Their choice! Their Karma.

With all of this spoken at the outset, You will be Blessed, as I delve more deeply, … to **clearly know the distinction between two fundamental intensities of Love**. Simply spoken, … **Conditional Love,** residing at the Third and Fifth Dimensional levels (3-D and 5-D), is entangled with the demands Ego, … in contrast to **Unconditional Love,** a quintessentially nurturing pure energy of Heart, completely free from all conditions of Ego. When released by a Giver, Unconditional Love, (UL), requires no reciprocity, as in 'Love Me Back too', etc. I realize with My full Compassion, … this is a huge leap of faith and consciousness within any Human Dimension. **BE comforted, that UL energy, highly refined and seated, *will live and float* *within you* and/or outwardly, as your Blessed Giver's Gift!**

21

Underlying Elements

As We begin and delve into the *Elements of True Compassion,* you will recognize the importance of these *underlying foundations. Here are the moving parts to proceed. To* simply make shallow assertions to the Universe in declaration of who you are will hardly suffice to align you with the necessary Elements of Compassion … energies you need to source and to gift this fine Spiritual Blessing as the Giver.

The basis of *True Compassion Elements* *is cast with a mind-set of Love, the Gift of Love, and Oneness in the process, an inflexible choice to engage without judgement, to maintain your neutrality, and to offer this Blessing delivered from within your paygrade.*

I will summarize these Elements as:

> *Love as a Giver*
> *Oneness of 'Being'*
> *Visceral connection*
> *Choices of the Giver*
> *Neutrality and non-judgement*
>   *of the Giver*
> *Boundaries of the Giver*
> *Forgiveness that surrounds*
> *Blessing from the Giver*

Now, let Me assist you with a preparatory conditioning of your mindset. As you see, this is an interlocking network of Spiritual imperatives ... all that deserve sharp focus. You will also find <u>these basics and more discussed in depth throughout My other books delivered through Lah Rahn Ananda.</u>

==Have you noticed that *absolutes* unconditionally embrace the Truth which never changes?==
(Master chuckles ... mmmmmmm)

Approach to Compassion Giving

When your consciousness is *aligned* to navigate the course of True Compassion Giving, you will possess *abilities to effortlessly and Lovingly float your energy gift into the consciousness of the object Receiver ... with your gift having been delivered as <u>you</u> have then consciously chosen.*

Alright!

==**Now comes the tricky part**== ... the corollary to the process of applying the Elements ... intricately coupled with this marvelous game of Compassion Giving.

You must now recognize that as Humans, both Giver and Receiver are inevitably exposed to the inherent circumstance at hand ... *and will therefore have <u>certain varying levels of feelings and emotions surrounding the process</u>.* And these chakra-destined energies land where they will and must be allowed to inflow as they will.

25

==Your job is to handle and process these emotions in a wise and aligned manner.== Many details of such aligned processes and actions are described in My books, **VICTORY FOR THE SOUL,** *Relationships That Work*, and **THE SAINT GERMAIN CHRONICLES COLLECTION,** *A Journey Into Practical Spirituality* ... *channled through* Gordon Corwin II aka Lah Rahn Ananda, Amazon 2016-2022.

And, ... moving along ... to further complicate matters in your Earth School, the *Duality on Earth* gets mixed into this pot ... often tempting you to choose sides, be partial, make judgements, and meticulously etch these into your *precious storehouse of resulting opinions, dutifully guarded by your Ego!* What a kettle of fish we have here! Such are lessons of the Earth School, <u>now in session</u>! (Master chuckles ...)

==**The *objective and requirements*** as a Compassion Giver are that you *transcend any possible emotional chaos and step for now into your super-Human shoes as a Giver Of True Compassion. Yes, this is an advanced assignment, I acknowledge.*==

And Yes, I also admit, this will take massive powers of discipline and transformation ... all serving you well throughout other parts of your Spiritual journey ahead. There will be *Ego temptations* with your feelings and possible sympathy in play, opinions that seek to gain ground, thoughts of taking sides, urges to join into grief-supporting sorrow and countless more. You will be continuously tested!

We Above have observed in Ones lacking preparatory grounding in their Approach to Compassion, that they become so immersed in the Receiver's plight that they themselves drown in the morass and sorrow they seek to mitigate with Compassion.

Forgiveness of Self

At this point, be prepared to forgive yourself if this need surfaces … ready to realign yourself and to forgive any and all lurking thoughts, judgements, or opinions surrounding the circumstance. You are Human. And, … you have a free-will choice to transcend these temptations. Act here and now use *your abilities as a Spiritual Observer*!

As you move through this process, remember to forgive yourself if you stumble on the block , … and *remember the all-important self-correction!* This is another tricky part, … to train yourself to be self-disciplined, recognize your own triggers and signs, and put in the corrections! (And make them stick! … Master chuckles …) Now you are on track and re-set to engage with integrity in the **sourcing of True Compassion.**

Remember, the energy of Compassion comes from within Your consciousness as the source, And concurrently, You are NOT the Judge and the Jury!

Here at this point in the 'process' you are fully aligned and grounded in the energy field you propose to create and deliver. You are now committed, …. You are engaged ... You are prepared in alignment.

> *As a Giver with Love, with your visceral connection, neutrality, and non-judgement … all comfortably nested in your aura, you float an energy healing into the consciousness of the Receiver, … holding their Heart(s) with the greatest of care … all wrapped in ease and grace.*

When you are contemplating My words, be open to this marvelous energy-sourcing opportunity of the Human Heart, a special role that awaits your full engagement.

You will discover, as you progress here, that energies of Compassion transport a unique version of Love, perhaps contrasting with your otherwise familiar or preconceived romantic or carnal notions about Love. (Master 'Hummmmm')

Being of Oneness

Once you allow your Ego-self to surrender to the real You, … and to get out of your own way, … your true Loving-Self can magically emerge, … and this *Being of Oneness* is truly positioned to be the Giver of Compassion, selflessly offering a Gift of Blessing … all for the taking!

TUNING UP YOUR VIBRATIONS

~ Applied Spirituality from Saint Germain ~

__EGO Behavior__ *compared with*	__Your Highest-Self Choices__
"My small story is what counts!" Over dramatizes. Is selfishly focused, ignoring Unity consciousness.	**Overcomes EGO's burning indulgence.** Replaced with *aligned self-choices for highest good.*
Ego confuses its small story with Reality! Indulges in *fear-based behavior*, including anger.	*Learns, applies, and remembers* life's lessons. *Embraces this process with empathy and overshining fear of* change.
Strives to be "important". The BIG shot! Greedy!	**Knows Joy** through *humility and helpfulness.*
"I'm always right" attitude. Arrogant. Believes Ego's *opinion* is correct! Ignores Human fallibility. Re-enforces a sagging self-esteem by denial.	**Seeks Truth, applying the merit of different perspectives** to each moment of every day life. Replaces denial with reality and self-integrity!
My opinion, i.e., "*my* truth", IS *the* Truth!!! "There are no other possibilities but mine!"	**Discerns the** *difference* between their belief system and *Universal/ law / Truth.*
Self-Aggrandizes. *Dominates* selfishly to over- ride or restrict others' Free-will choices. Makes untenable excuses. Projects the blame onto another one/thing. "It's someone else's fault". *Avoids accountability and responsibility.*	Seeks Mastery of Spirit's teachings of Truth. See The Saint Germain Chroniclers Collection. **Knows Truth and accepts reality with Joy.** **Pacifies an untamed EGO into submission into its rightful role.** Promotes harmony.
Complains about *unfulfilled expectations*. Demands *immediate* satisfaction! Prefers *complaining* to implementing solutions! Gets "stuck" on irreconcilable issues	**Demonstrates patience by shrinking EGO's** stature, now relegated *to take a back seat*.
	Seeks out and implements creative Win-win solutions. Replaces complaints without squandering energy. **Expresses gratefulness. Sees Blessings!**
Obsesses about dissatisfactions.	
Escalates frustration into anger and hate. Enjoys being angry; regards as acceptable! *Impatience* accelerates into anger. *Believes anger or hate get the best results,*	**Utilizes Saint Germain's** healing techniques as presented in His book 'Victory for the Soul, Relationships That Work', Gordon Corwin II -Lah Rahn Ananda, Amazon.
Uses anger to "bully" others, often hiding *fear*. Promotes conflict and greed. Seeks revenge. Unable and or unwilling to *recognize emotions*.	**Recognizes own behavior** in real-time. *Elevates negative emotions,* raising them up into Neutral or Positive zones. Is accountable for Own Behaviors.
Satisfied staying stuck in Egos's versions *of unlearned life's lessons.*	**Fully ENJOYS the Mastery and rewards of Aligned Actions and Higher Dimensions.** **Discovers the Human Condition!** **Transcends the Human Illusion!!**
Attached to Ego as a prisoner of its own device.	**Aligns consciousness with Universal / Divine Law,** *freeing their Highest-Self to BE.*

"To Truly Be or not to BE is Your Question". Saint Germain

Through Lah Rahn Ananda 05/2010 Rev. 07/2022

TRANSCENDING INTO UNCONDITIONAL LOVE

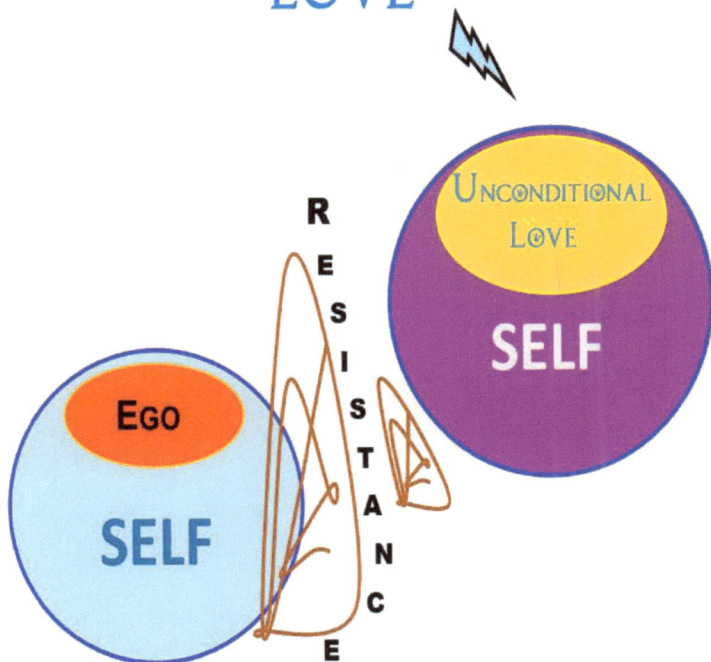

HIGHER
DIMENSIONAL
ONENESS

separation

TRUE
SELF

EGO

SELF

Yes, potential receivers, <u>the Objects of Compassion,</u> may well exercise their *free-will right of choice* to do as they will, … a situation <u>beyond the</u> <u>boundaries of your concern</u> and role as the Giver.

Object-Receiver individuals, as you shall see, may choose the embrace of Compassion as a welcome wave of nurturing energy oncoming in a timely way, … **or** … choose to remain in whatever state they find themselves, passing up this gift, as a shadow in the night. *(Some Ones do unfortunately resist. <u>They find pay offs in</u> their resistance and/or addictions to pain).*

Detachment with Love

As the Giver, wisely be aware of your role as a <u>nurturer</u> offering heart-Love to be received or not.

Be aware of the boundary limitations of your gift, where you might attempt to cure the irreversible ... possibly a fortune dispensed by the Universe, above your pay grade. Either way, Unconditional Love can prevail if there is an open doorway for Compassion to find its mark.

Emotional tendering becomes available to Ones vulnerable enough to open their doorways.

A Love Infusion

Consider your gift of True Compassion and its possible receipt … as a Heart-Love infusion wrapped in ease and grace of the moment.

About Boundaries of the Giver

With your boundaries *wisely in place,* as I will describe, you are enabled, nonetheless, to enjoy the sunshine and joy of *your own life-stream*.

As you may see by now, Compassion has its boundaries, Folks, for Ones aware and awake to the pitfalls that lie beyond True Compassion. Many a well-meaning and Loving Spiritual Chela, unaware of the boundaries of which I speak, would further extend their energies into Sympathy, … where *they cross prudent boundaries and take on energies of the Object person or circumstance or both, often to become embroiled and entangled themselves, sharing the Object's pain, misery, and grief, etc.*

In plain language, so there is absolute clarity foremost for you, … **without your boundaries consciously anchored in place, you yourself risk a devastating collapse into whatever grief, sadness, and hopelessness, etc. the Object may radiate**. This collapse could easily drown you in the muck, as a disoriented, ungrounded person along with the Object and its circumstances. **If you allow this mistake**, you too may likely become personally entangled, viscerally overwhelmed, to then vibrate in tune with the very low fallen energies you are **intending to Bless and uplift with the Love of True Compassion!** Best you reread!

Such sympathetic One's *Egos have chosen to engage*, … perhaps not consciously, … *to sympathetically attach themselves, their judgements, and opinions, ... to the issue, person, etc. at hand.*

And guess what? Here, You too would then be hooked. You too may then become a *candidate, desperate* for the very Compassion that you seek to give!! **Yes or yes?** *(Master chuckles hhaaa haaaaaaaa).*

41

Such Givers have been drawn into the mix by crossing a boundary then leading into their own Sympathy! Now, their Ego's judgements, opinions, illusions, and victimization to the Human condition land in *their own arena*. Such Givers have allowed their own boundaries of which I speak to collapse. This is a *fine line to walk*, I grant you.

Givers ignoring needed boundaries will now have their own circumstance of triggers, emotions, further choices, and actions to resolve! Such tasty morsels await engaged drama queens of Sympathy!

By now do you see the vast contrast between Compassion with its boundaries and Sympathy?

We Above often observe scenarios of Givers becoming entrapped in their own plight, caught in the drama of the web they weave. (Master ... humor chuckles about Drama).

Envision in comic relief, if you will, a stage play with characters depicting various players in the above drama. You fill in your own blanks. I write few plays in my current role as Maja Chohan.

Self-Compassion

Along the same vein, a wise Giver of Compassion will be aware of *Self-Compassion*. The short story is to administer to yourself, when you sense the need, ... a quantum of Compassion that is merit-worthy as I have outlined. In concert with this vibration, again be aware of tangling yourself up in the *sympathy* aspect, a plight that We see from Above that can easily further lead you to be the *victim*.

43

Mastery of the Self-Compassion process has bountiful rewards ... highlighted with peace of mind in a troubled World. Nota Bene. Enough said.

And I realize, Oh My! More elucidation will likely give My Dear Lah Rahn a typer's-cramp ... one which would merit your unconditional Compassion, within some boundary awareness, of course. (*More chuckle*)

Alright!

All of this being spoken, ... beware here, as We are approaching a crossroads. I'm speaking of your essential knowingness and intuition coming into play here. This 'sense' will allow you to pin-point, ... *without judgement* ... situations of *potential compassion that qualify ... or not.*

Your free-will choice with observation with non-judgement is highly tested at this crossroad. Some situations you *will* deem worthy of your Compassion. However, where do you draw the line? Which fork of the crossroad will you take?

Let's cut to the chase. Clearly, circumstances, predicaments, and negative outcomes need come under the magnifying glass.

For example, those situations which are the result of _deliberately_ harmful, _knowingly_ harmful actions, even though compulsions, addictions, etc. may be in play. These types of _accountable actions_, clearly out of Divine alignment, deserve your attention as _undeserving_ of Compassion. Know that Karma will have its way!

Humans, (with rare exceptions, I grant you) do, at a deep level ... of even the _lowest parts of the 3rd Dimension_, ... realize the distinction between 'positive and negative,' 'fundamentally right and wrong' (within the rules of the society in which they live), 'good and evil', 'constructive versus destructive', etc.

***

Look over your list for _Compassion candidates_ with great care, My Friends! Your Free-will is being tested mightily ... <u>choose as you will. And shoulder the consequences of your choices</u>! _Unworthy endorsements of Compassion can carry heavy Karma ... placed directly upon your shoulders! Nota Bene!_

***

47

Be clear that you alone, yes you, are responsible for your actions of <u>Compassion-worthy choices</u>.

Chelas will cleverly attempt to dodge the gaff here by *asking Spirit what to do* … by asking Spirit if the situation is Compassion-worthy or not, … *by asking Spirit to make their free-will choice for them.*

<u>Spirit does NOT make your free-will choices for you!</u> You alone are on the hook. If you ask Spirit and if you hear or believe you are told that Spirit is responding with your free-will choice for you, ... ***<u>you are sadly drowned in the illusion of your EGO</u>.***

<mark>This self-deception of false-listening becomes your responsibility, burden and Karma.</mark>

Do I have your Attention?

<u>Do not believe in the popular illusion</u> that you can ask Us in the Ascended Realm (or whomever your ***<u>Ascended Guides</u>*** may be) to choose for you!

If you want to evolve and span the upward rungs of the Spiritual ladder, you need to <mark>learn to habitually *contact your Highest-self,* … to ask, to listen and to receive accurately the Wisdom you have gleaned over this and past lifetimes.</mark>
This is part of your life-experience training. Yes, there may be mistakes and from these you will learn if you are wise and not repeat. Have you heard of the Earth School?

Those in the 5ᵗʰ Dimension are fully engaged in this learning communication process, one which is front and center!

Those who seek and receive admission to the 5ᵗʰ, the 7ᵗʰ Dimension and the 9ᵗʰ Dimension have by now keenly learned _the lessons of distinguishing what and from whom they hear_ ... with their Ego parts, distinct from their Highest-self, and distinct from pure Spirit.

**Your upward progress in Ascending through the Dimensions depends greatly upon accurate communication with Ourselves Above, and faulty practices are deal-breakers for your evolution.**

Thus, when in your process of _dispensing_ this heartful energy of Compassion, ... fine Givers of _merit-worthy Compassion will clearly recognize the voice of their Egos in distinct and abundant contrast to Our voices from Above._

Love and Compassion

As the energy of Compassion is dispensed and received, a beautiful Oneness is created, a vibration born of pure Love.

Prepared to Serve

A lasting quality is connected to this unique wave of energy, and it adheres to Ones genuinely immersed in this Heart-sourced process of *Being in the Oneness of All*. True Compassion Givers in action have thus earned a Spiritual credential of sorts, vibrational stripes sewn onto their sleeves, an insignia, a cachet to be acknowledged and admired by those onlooking from the outside in, from various Dimensions in which observers may dwell.

Fear not of an isolated Ego' loss when Oneness is close at hand. The beauty of Oneness seen as a wholeness, *without Separation*, enriches the wonder of your Humanity. **Experiencing Oneness far surpasses the reach of an Ego's fear.** Devoid of Ego, your True-self is further unveiled as you allow your conscious belief system and your Highest-self to be aligned as Blessed by the Laws of the Universe. *(A low-flying hawk is observed overhead and its shrill cry pierces the air).*

When this fully wonderous experience of wholeness touches your heart, ... when this experience of your destiny to be in *Oneness consciously rests within you*, You will feel **The Light of Compassion** resting with joy in your Heart-space.

In this state, with your unconditional gratefulness, expressed and returned to Spirit and the Universe itself, … in these moments of ease and grace, … you will feel Blessed yourself.

My Dearest Friends,
as you journey forward, … be keenly aware of that common thread of manifestation, deeply woven throughout the depths of My teachings. I speak about the act of injecting the *coefficient of aligned* *action into your daily Spiritual practice.* *Ever so sadly, Dear Hearts, this quintessential act* *is commonly overlooked*, … blunting if not diffusing the evolvement impact of the magnificent life's lesson We lovingly orchestrate along your Dharmic life path.

Gift yourself with the Blessing of *regular, daily,* *and hourly application of the Wisdom I offer,* actively embracing … beyond merely idly contemplating or just knowing … as you *integrate* *routine into your daily Earth life*. For the sake of your Soul, I beseech you to garner your courage now and seize the day,
My good people of Earth.

Expressing timely gratefulness is a clincher for the wise. Synchronicities are catalyzed by expressing gratefulness unto Spirit in the moment … in your real time.

With this awareness in action, Compassion will live in you as a default habit pattern, to be deeply felt and shared when circumstances merit this Blessing.

Kindly remember that Compassion is linked with Forgiveness, as together they synthesize and deliver heartful energies, serving together as inseparable Partners of Love.

Differing opinions, varied belief systems, cultures, and more can cause clashes that resist … actions from the Objects of Compassion energy. These can remain so, or can *be dissolved and reconciled at the conscious Heart level as Egos would allow.*

Treat yourself to an additional helping of **Forgiveness and Compassion** *by reading and ingesting Chapter 10 in one of My latest books* ~~Victory For The Soul, Relationships that Work,~~ *Saint Germain and Gordon Corwin II, 2022 Amazon.*

The Wisdom in this book's Chapter 10 will further enlighten you **with supplemental perspectives** about *True Compassion, Merging Love Into Oneness. Enjoy!*

Unconditional Compassion, thusly deployed <u>and</u> freely received by the Object of Compassion … becomes an integral pillar in the foundation of that bridge spanning from *separation into Oneness* …. a Divine Cosmic space where you rightfully belong.

Note that a Soul Ascending from a Human Earthly incarnation is analogous to launching an Earth vehicle out of the Sun's (solar) gravitational orbit, and thus out of this restrictive gravitational field, into Cosmic Dimensions. *Soul healing and Soul travel* is easily then orchestrated by Spirit as part of the purification and Dharmic reassignment process above the Astral plane.

Recognizing <u>and</u> accepting <u>and</u> adhering to the axioms of evolvement will open future gateways to *potentially* launch you into a new Soul orbit beyond present Human comprehension...*higher Human Dimensions of which I speak shall reward you with a new outlook upon living your days as Aligned and Spiritually worthwhile on Earth.* And, … will <u>have delivered unto you a new and magnificent leg of your of Earth Freedom Journey to stand upon!</u>

> *The shoes you then wear to climb the Spiritual ladder toward Ascension thru the Human Dimensions will be tightly laced with ribbons of ease and grace signifying an aligned life-path worthy of living.*

The stage is set. You hold the Spiritual tools nested in MY writings. Higher Dimensions await.

Progressive stages of Higher Dimensions of consciousness lie beyond for the dedicated and courageous. Although the air is rare when the road gets narrower, aligned living yields you many many additional ripe fruits of miraculous Human living filled with a life of joy, Love, peace, and Human happiness. I speak the Truth.

Beyond the 3rd Dimensional plane, *where 'hope' is expanded to include action,* lies The 5th Dimension of Love and Higher Healing, The 7th Dimension of Liberation, and The 9th Dimension of Purity and Unconditional Love. Take heart of your bright future.

Prepared to Serve

Once the elements I Offer are well seated in your consciousness, You are prepared to enter the Domain of True Compassion … to source the nurturing energy of today's transmission.

This heartful *dance of True Compassion,* *with you as the aligned Giver, positions you for rising to higher Dimensional levels of vibration further along the path of your Spiritual Journey.*

You have the keys. Unlocking and purging those Ego parts of you that no longer serve will allow your path to be illuminated as I have spoken, coupled with a fresh and new sense of personal *Freedom* beyond your current recognition.

Doorways will open along this delightful path. Ease and grace will dress your life. New horizons will appear in the form of those Higher Dimensional rewards ahead offered by the 5th, 7th, and 9th Dimensions of Higher Human consciousness that await your entry,

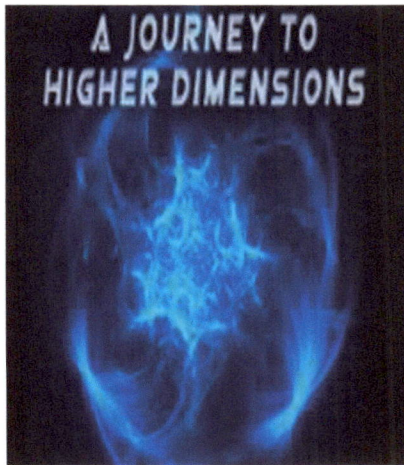

*When I thus sprinkle your journey
with My embolding guidance,
be comforted to know there is a touchstone
energy nestled within the Ascended Realm ...
awaiting your presence. Merged together as
One, Sananda and Lady Nada stand ready to
gently hold your heart within the nurturing
space of True Compassion, escorting you to
the door of Oneness that awaits.*

ॐ ॐ

In Conclusion

As You shed layers of Ego armour that cling, and as you open your 3rd eye to gaze beyond the reality of Human illusion and behold the Truths of Divine Reality, you shall enter this New Paradigm of Compassion that holds Cosmic promise beyond your current belief system, Dear Friends.

Join with Me and the entire Realm of Ascended Masters that serve Humanity, … as We serve to accelerate your Spiritual journey, … ultimately destined to place you in Our arms. We Above await your full engagement and offer Our True Compassion to You as You progress and pass the milestones leading to your Spiritual Mastery and Ascension.

We Ascended Above Lovingly offer to you these possibilities of evolvement as Being of Free-will choice. Now, walking the path to greater happiness and Mastery of Human living for yourself and Mankind is in your hands, My Dear Friends.

I trust you will answer My call and rise to this momentous occasion of truly holding the Quality of True Compassion in your Heart throughout this lifetime and beyond. The choice is yours to answer the call of your Soul.

With My Fondest Blessings to All

Saint Germain

Through Lah Rahn Ananda aka Gordon Corwin II

Be A Friend of Change.

The ADDENDUM pages that follow in this book are My special gift to you. You can make this gift so with your free-will choice ... if you are wise. **CHANGE**, an absolute essential for you to employ in the process of learning Compassion Giving. The name of this writing to follow is **"Friend of Change'**, ... these pages present a full transcription of a live, channeled public event in the year 1998, where your fellow Chelas and public attendees are interacting directly with Me as Saint Germain, asking their Spiritual questions and receiving answers.

Enjoy the dialogue and the energy!

The Bells

RING THE BELLS THAT
CAN RING!

ENJOY THOSE BELLS
THAT RANG!

BE GRATEFUL FOR THE
HARMONY!

LOOSEN YOUR GRIP!

REMEMBER LOVE!

GRATITUDE

To My Dear Friends walking your path. As you allow Ascended Spirit to enlighten and expand the veins of your consciousness, I invite you to please join me in reciprocating the deepest possible gratitude for the very wonders of the Creator's Universe itself, and for the infinite brilliance embodied in this interconnecting structure throughout the highest dimensions of Universal Consciousness.

God and Spirit have so ingeniously interwoven, as ONE, an amazing, infinitely organized hierarchical structure of Ascended Beings and timeless wisdom, allowing us on Earth to receive purifying transmissions from Above in real time, as they are continuously and effortlessly sent to Humanity. In my Channeling and role as a Partner of Spirit, I AM most grateful to serve as a minute part of this wondrous network of Spirit and Light, receiving for you the highest vibrational Octaves of Universal Truth. In more simple terms, this is gratefulness for delivery of our Divinely guided toolset for living 'The Grand Process' in this lifetime of self-transformation, awake and aware.

You may know that individual Ascended Masters carry their own unique energy, style, and color, delivering that segment of the Whole, which is their Ray of assigned specialty. And yet, ironically, these Beings are fully aligned, integrated, amalgamated, and enfolded into the greater Whole as ONE. I AM personally grateful that this demonstration of transcended Oneness from Above displays doorways to Unity consciousness and then God Consciousness for all of us.

My dream is for you to find these Books and Discourses to be your Personal Spiritual Guidelines, leading you to experience the perfection of God's Grace, as you walk through your own doorways arched with inset stones of timeless wisdom. Over the past 25 years, the many books and discourses I have channeled with Saint Germain also contain energies emanating from *several* other

Ascended Masters to all of whom I AM immensely grateful. Please join me in the most heartful acknowledgement of: Lords Saint Germain, El Morya, Buddha, Hilarion, Mighty Victory, Jesus Sananda, Lady Portia, Lady Nada, Mother Mary, Archangels Michael, Zadkiel, Gabriel, the now several Angelic Legions serving this Vortex, and countless enlightened Beings, standing to serve when called. May Spirit's Grace gently crown the consciousness of incarnated devotees as you all walk your unique paths of discovery and quest into Mastery of this lifetime.

Many Blessings to you,

Love, Lah Rahn aka Gordon Corwin II

75

LIGHT FOR THE SOUL

El Morya Transmission

Through Lah Rahn Ananda

Prayer of Divine Moments

Lead me, oh my sweet Lord, to choose thy bounty forever, for I know it is my destiny. Let me now hear your inspirations' love that guides me to make the most from each of our moments together,

for I AM one with Thee.

As your child I stand in awe of the Divined free-will gift bestowed upon me and entrusted into my care. Guide me to heartfully know thy will as I carefully choose each of my new moments' beginnings. My right choices shall be the walk of my dharma that I demonstrate in full view of ALL,

for I AM one with Thee.

May I forever embrace the lessons of my moments which I know embody my own choices. Grace me, Lord, with true perception of my every moment, though parts be bittersweet as I may choose to perceive. Let me see that I am blessed by all of my lessons, for I AM one with You.

Oh give me the awakened remembrance of my own Divine Self that reveals the true identity of Me to me in your likeness,
        for I AM one with YOU.

Let my will be your will forever and forever, oh my sweet Lord. Guide the steps of my walk to be trustworthy in the eyes of ALL. I pray to ignite the violet flame in the altar of my heart within each one of my newly treasured and joyfully shared moments with Thee. I AM your inspired instrument of Divine heart that chooses in love our moments together,

        for I AM so in love with

                YOU
        Oh my sweet Lord my CREATOR

El Morya

Through Lah Rah Ananda
just for you 2001

Being

Living

Knowing

Intake

Inquiry

The Teachings

Saint Germain's Tool Box

Lati Kahn 2023

81

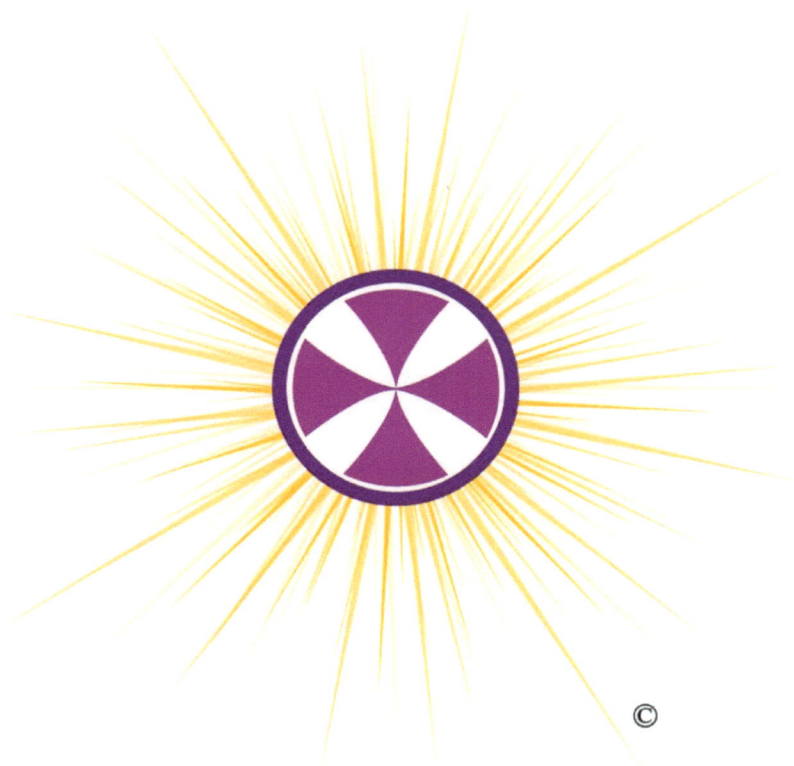

©

Friend of Change

Spoken by Ascended Master

𝔖aint 𝔊ermain

A Channeled Live Dictation
Through Lah Rahn Ananda
Circa July 1998

This work was taped live during a public Sacred Love
Gathering of Souls in Oceanside, California USA
who came together in love and surrendered dedication to
witness Spirit, hear their words, and feel the essence of the
Ascended Masters speaking.

The Master speaking upon this occasion was Lord Saint
Germain, Chohan of the Aquarian Age, delivering loving
support to individuals dedicated to mastering their Human
lives in Divine alignment in *this* lifetime. Neither the audience
nor the channel had prior knowledge of the message to come
nor the subject which was to be addressed.

Many were surprised and taken that day by their experience, which in the years to follow turned out to be shockingly true and accurate as each participant was to discover. All who were present are now most grateful, since this work remains timeless and true today and beyond.

Lah Rahn Ananda continues channeling to this day in February, 2023 now in Earth-Partnership with Master Saint Germain, co-authoring and publishing several Saint Germain books including *The Saint Germain Chronicles Collection*, *Victory For The Soul*, *Rising Above*, *True Compassion*, Merging Love into Oneness, *and other available unpublished works.*

As for you, my Dear Reader, this is your timely opportunity also to choose to become an equally full participant in this and future Masterful work. When you inflow and comprehend these energies, as well as the training in the imbedded catalytic workbooks for your growth, it is Masterfully intended that you be taken and uplifted by your proactive embodiment and practice of this wisdom as a *Friend of Change.*

๛ ๛

Event Begins and
Saint Germain begins to speak

"I AM overjoyed to speak to the hearts of each one of you this day. You are my flag carriers. You are my standard bearers ... standard bearers of the Aquarian Age. As Lord St. Germain I Am indeed overjoyed that each of you would arrange your circumstances this day to be in this presence of the Holy Spirit.

In the Ascended Realm We are, so to speak, clapping our ethereal hands together ... although we have no more hands. As we became unattached, we gave those up, much in the same way as all of you are becoming unattached to your minds' belief systems of how things should be ... of how things should turn out ... and of how you should have your way above all else. And then giving all that back to Spirit.

In these times upon Planet Earth, change and then more change you shall see, and as I have spoken before, ... change shall become your middle name.

Now, I come to you this day, to nurture your ego consciousness in a way that these parts of you will be able to step aside so that YOU, as standard bearers of Spirit, can indeed, walk your walk, dance your dance, find your passion ... rather I need say remember your passion, ... and then each BE in the flow of your Dharma's life force.

As always, you have the opportunity for choice – choice of either maintaining the *status quo* with things held in place as best as you can exactly as they are, or of welcoming inevitable change. No risk – so you think.

No burden – your mind may say that. Just get by and cling. Survive and keep things in the status quo. You might even say that the Ego consciousness enjoys being frozen in place ...especially if it feels it is playing a winning game.

And then the Soul-self of you comes forth in a very heartfelt, gracious way as it has, to bring you to this gathering today ... and your <u>Highest-self says,</u> ... "Yes, I Am in charge. I Am in charge from now on and I Am sorry, my dear Ego, if you are offended. I Am very compassionate. For it is true that I have removed your crown and I have placed it upon my head now as the Grand Higher Self and I ask that you as the self ... the small self-centered Ego consciousness vibrating in the lower four bodies of the human being ... *I ask now that you (ego) ...now lie down.* Thank you very much for your past contribution to Me ...as <u>your Higher-self wears the crown.</u>

(Higher-self continues) ...

Now it is my turn – I Am choosing to live, think, converse, act, walk and be One with the Holy Spirit. And, I will honor you ... I will honor you my dear Ego as a very important part – as my ally – as my *surrendered* ally.

(Saint Germain) You see, when you lie down in surrender and when you give yourself over to your Higher-self, then it has the benefit of your expertise, your services. Higher-self is now my loving and surrendered steward."

So speaks the Soul voice of you, to manage, console, and court a crest-fallen EGO-mind.

And the voice of the Soul continues: ...
"Now it is true in the past you (Ego) have been able to have your way. And just to make you feel good while I Am transitioning into my light, into a vessel that can hold Spirit's light, I will allow you some of your desires – yes, I certainly will. I will nurture you, I will hold you as I Am gaining more and more insight, more wisdom, more surrender, and more detachment ... I will nurture you. So let's strike a little bargain here ... I will nurture you.

And knowing this, I ask that you, my fine separated Ego consciousness part ... I ask that you become *my friend* – so that, as you say, you get with the band wagon here – climb on board and together we shall make a fine, fine team, you and I. Let us be partners.

Let us be teammates in a fine little connected community of SELF. And I Am grateful beyond expression." (Higher-self stops).

Alright.

Saint Germain:

Now this could well be a conversation that you have with your Ego consciousness on an ongoing basis. For I promise you it will be required every now and then. Even among Our more surrendered ones, the ego consciousness will want to stand up and say its say at times. And when this occurs, of course, you have this conversation. You can well see in this scenario how your wishes and desires are apart from your needs. Your beliefs are apart from your knowing, distinct – one from the other.

You can see I Am tendering you so that you yourself can, ironically enough, nurture your Ego consciousness with love, and nurture it into surrender. Nurture it with love into its surrender. I can remember in many lifetimes of mine doing this very process and while it is true, some of my lifetimes ... especially in some of the last ... I was in company, consorting, associating, and serving of royalty – kings and queens alike – and I remember oh so well these conversations with my own ego at that time.

Now, I Am going to give you the punch line – I have tendered you long enough!

Today here, *We are tendering the Ego consciousness with Love – We are nurturing your Ego consciousness so that it can die. The separated part of the Ego needs to die. Remember the Shaman? Isn't it ironical that we are nurturing something that needs to die. Well, that's the game. That's the irony!*

When you embrace change, <u>as you are now asked</u>, and you are supported from the Ascended Realms to also embrace all now... *the ego consciousness is rather raw as it faces massive change, surrender, and its own death.*

After all, it has been dethroned – it has been uncrowned. *You are nurturing with love – embracing the Ego consciousness so that it can die ... so that you can <u>embrace change</u>. Affix this in your permanent consciousness as the days, weeks, and months ahead bring forth more and more change. Do not worry or fret about what changes are down the road. Let us orchestrate the future. More about this later on.*

As was spoken earlier today through this messenger, it is your privilege, it is your Divine power to be in co-creation with ourselves in the present moment without regard to the future or the past... *'in the present moment I do create'. In the past – excluding the present moment – there is no creation future.*

Do you see how that simplifies things for you? And the Ego mind says, yes, but what about all these things in the past? ... think present moment ... present moment.

> **O**nce in the Moment at present time,
>
> My Christed self I do align.
>
> In these moments of reverie,
>
> Up spring the joys I choose to be.

The Universe, Spirit, the Creator, however you wish to speak it, is undergoing enormous change. As the Creator evolves so do we evolve all together – Ascended Spirit, beings of earth, beings in other worlds – evolve together. We're moving – up and up. Evolution has no end.

And so as change is metered out to each and every one of you individually and through a collective, your choice is: Am I willing to be surrendered to that which the Universe hands me next – and hands me next – and then hands me next? Am I really willing to be surrendered to what the Universe hands me next? Think of it as a large stack of dinner plates where the Universe hands you one plate. You do what you do with it – and then you pick off another one off the stack.

And then it hands you another plate and you do what you do with that – thank you very much. And we hand you another plate, and so on.

And your mind thinks, well we're going to get to the bottom of the stack here and when we're at the bottom of the stack we can go back to the *status quo.*

'It's finished and there shall be no more changes!'

Well, it's a little trick that's been played on you.
The plates are sitting on a spring in a well and when
you take the last plate off the top up pops another plate,
and another plate and another one, ... in a constant
streaming flow of life's lessons in evolution perpetual.

As Lord Saint Germain of the Seventh Ray and
as the Designated Master of the Aquarian Age I ask
you, each and every one, to come into partnership with
me regarding *change* – embracing your Ego so that
you can erase separated status-quo desires, and let the
changes be all wrapped in love. I know you see that
without change we are stuck with the status quo upon
Planet Earth.

There's an old saying ... I won't say it exactly as
some people say it, but it goes something like; If it isn't
broken, don't fix it – just leave things the same as they
are. Would you say that supports the status quo?

Well, all of you must know by now that
consciousness upon Planet Earth on the collective and
on the individual levels, is so very unintegrated and it
does need your Love and attention in co-operation with
ourselves. So as you choose to regard change with
Love, what's actually happening is that you approach
your life in a higher vibration – you actually vibrate at a
higher frequency – *the frequency of Love vibrates
differently than the frequency of fear.*

Is it not interesting that we always get back to the basics. The human being vibrates in love and the human ...the divining human ... the D*ivining* human...all humans are Divining ... some just don't know it yet, ... the D*ivining human* vibrates in the beginning at the survival level – in the first chakra ... at the base of the spine.

Survival vibration is one of fear. Our process is to work together to raise the consciousness of the Divining humanity wherever you may be from the level of human into the level of *human being*. Know well that distinction of human... evolved... to the level of *human being*. Beyond The Human Illusion, folks!

So are we asking of you to be super-human? Indeed we are!! I confess ... being super- human to the point where every circumstance and situation that you encounter is encountered on the level ... the vibratory level, ... of unconditional love. Alright.

Close your eyes for a moment. I Am going to assist you. Close your eyes – if you have anything on your lap take it off your lap and uncross your arms and legs. I Am going to allow Lah Rahn Ananda to stay where he is, although he can arrange himself in a little more optimum pattern.

Visualize in your consciousness change and a fear
... be honest with yourself ... a fear that you have had ...
a recent one about a change ... something you're not too
sure about and you feel the willies in your stomach ... in
the pit of your gut...not too comfortable. Whatever
other emotion you might have, bring this up in your
consciousness – a fear of change – something you know
is up ... and it's not optional. Feel the feeling of it.
Feel where it resonates in your body ... the cellular level
of fear. Alright, now hold that for a moment ... just
hold that right where it is.

Now I want you to open up your brow chakra
– your third eye – and out in front of that third eye
create a ball of golden white light. Bring it up on your
T. V. screen of your third eye – now intensify that light
– intensify it more.
So white that it becomes blinding ... it becomes so
blinding that you're starting to feel it out in the cells of
your body ... your createdness ... ***hold the light –
concentrate*** – if you don't concentrate then you'll lose
it ... hold the light – blinding white – a display of our
love – of our vibration in the Ascended
Realms.

Now, I want you to go back to where you were
and take that fear – center it over your spine – and
move it directly upwards up your spine ... up
through the heart chakra ... up through the throat chakra
– see the blue ... on up into the brow chakra ... through
the indigo ... now take that fear and move it right into
the center of the light ... just let it dissipate into the
Light.

105

Notice the feeling you now have in your body ... in the Light... *feel the peace ... feel the relief and the freedom. I ask that you remember this process –a process of giving it back, as you would say, giving fear back to Spirit. And I Bless each and every one of you with this gift. It would be wise if you remember it and use it.*

Alright, I think that's about all you can handle for this day. I will be most pleased to <u>answer any questions that you may have before I go.</u>

Participant: Was your last incarnation as the Wonderman of Europe?

St. Germain: That is correct. You see, at that time I was already a member of the Ascended Realm and it was to be that I come back another time ... one more time ...and that is not to say that I do not come and visit you now ...but I Am speaking of a fully incarnated life-time ... and to bring light at a particular time when Earth needed Light so very much.

We were in change at that time also ... kings, queens and royalty ... and it had become known that that was no longer working for Me ... and we found another source rather ...   you found *another source through your own evolution*. And then churches came more into popularity as royalty was moved off to the side. Thank you for your question.

Participant: You are welcome.

St. Germain: Thank you, it is my pleasure. Anyone else before I go?

Participant: What is my weakness? My weakest moment?

St. Germain: Your weakest moment ... and this goes for each and every one of you ... your weakest moment is when you choose to be your Ego self, simply put.
The details ... the tentacles that hang down from that, *are your assignments as we hand you different circumstances* ... as you create and draw to the energies of different circumstances – and different aspects of you get honed, initiated and taught their lessons. Do you see?

Participant: Yes, I'm noticing that during those initiations and those times, there's just a still quiet place that remains even though all other things are happening.

St. Germain: What is that place?

Participant: It is Spirit.

St. Germain: That's right. So you see you are really two people ... you are two people, and in the process of your evolution you go back and forth from being one and the other ... now you're Spirit ... now you're back in this lower human vibration ... and now you're Spirit ... and now you're not. And as you evolve, there's more of this as Spirit and less of the lower vibrations.

And as you evolve there's more of this and less of that (St. Germain uses Lah Rahn to gesture two opposites) ... and then it all comes to here (gestures the HEART). And now my Beloved Ones, when you reach this point you are ready to be *taken*. How does that feel? You are ready to be *taken.*

When you shuck this lower part in your consciousness there is a giving and a taking – you all spoke of this earlier today – and when you give up enough of this lower part, then you are ready to be given and to be taken. That is hope ... that is our gift.

Participant: **When you are ready to be taken,** would that mean your Ascension would take you out of your body or would you remain and become a Master of the Planet?

St. Germain: **Thank you, that's a very good question** – it shows that you are looking forward – it's where I want you. The answer is it could be both ... it could be one or the other. Many ones that are ready to be taken are left upon this plane to remain into our service. Many are taken to the other side. It depends really upon the Soul agreement that you have with ourselves. It also depends upon your choice at that time ... for you see when you become Divined, you are One with our consciousness and when you are One you know these things. So it's up to your higher self to commune with ourselves and decide... when an appropriate time comes along ... when a juncture is reached.

Participant: There's no way you can tell, though?

St. Germain: **That would be giving it away.** You see, I would be shortchanging you to do your work for you.

In any event, if you are truly **taken**, *others who are keenly perceptive will observe this miracle and notice it long before you do.*

If *you announce* to the world your own Ascension, be assured it is actually your most untamed and unevolved ego part that is crying out for the Spiritual self- esteem that it sadly and pitifully lacks. An Ascended Being asked to remain now upon Mother Goddess Earth and serve the Holy Spirit for a period of Earth time, would simply not make such an announcement nor be allowed by our Realms to do so.

Humility is a supreme quality unconditionally required to gain entrance to the 5th and higher octave Dimensions.

Participant: Thank you, St. Germain.

St. Germain: You are most welcome and you are most loved.

Participant: I'd like to ask one more question in relation to the Soul.

St. Germain: One more.

Participant: **Have there been any physical Ascensions lately or have people left their bodies on the Earth?**

St. Germain: Whether or not a Being leaves the body behind depends upon a number of factors which We Above decide at the time ... it depends in part on the needs of the collective at that time with respect to this being as to how it will serve once the Spirit has Ascended ... how it will serve – or not serve – to leave a body behind. There have been few Ascensions in the last decade.

We are optimistic that this number will augment exponentially in the coming 2 decades on Earth, and beyond as well.
Alright, I can't entertain your Egos too much more.

Participant: **What kind of physical Earth changes** is Mother Goddess Earth going to experience in the next month and what can we do to be there and heal her at that time?

St. Germain: **I will answer your question and before I do, I ask that you look at the first part of that question to see where it comes from?** (Pause)

Alright. Thank you. The physical changes that Mother Goddess Earth will experience are determined in the time and in the moment of the requirement, and the energies then move, stay still, transform, change shape ... *as they need change in the energy of that moment.*

Now with regard to the second part of your question, the healing, "what can I do"? What can we do to do our part to bring forth a healing here of Mother Goddess Earth? **Let me just say your very presence here today is a notable part of that healing. I applaud you all!**

When you go to Mother Goddess Earth in the morning before your day commences and you sit upon her and you do your daily meditation – you are healing Mother Goddess Earth. When you say your decrees heartfully ... as was done in this gathering ... you are healing Mother Goddess Earth.

Decreeing need be done by each one of you each and every day ... and remember it's possible to do it during your day when the forces of the Ego consciousness come forth and grab you by the throat ... just try and you will be amazed at the results.

Try it once and you may never ever stop. Say a small decree ... you are healing when you say decrees. When you are in prayer, you are healing the planet.

When you bring loving calmness to a situation of chaos, you heal the planet. When you interact with the angelic realms, you are healing the planet – it goes on and on. When you change to love over fear, you're healing the planet. And there are more and more of you – more and more of you gathering in these groups.

You have no idea how the number of groups that I source has increased in just the last couple of years...and We are most grateful, We are most grateful.

Ascended Spirit cannot do this without you ... *I want you to know that I love you* ... **I Am most appreciative of your keen attention today and the heartfulness that each one of you has brought to your other brothers and sisters and to this gathering. It has been most magnificent and my great pleasure.**

Thank you and good day".

Saint Germain slowly withdraws energy
from the Vortex.

𝕾aint 𝕲ermain

Through Lah Rahn Ananda aka
Gordon Corwin II
July 26, 1998, Oceanside, California

ACKNOWLEDGEMENTS

Once again, I Am overjoyed to acknowledge you who have contributed so much talent and Love to the Worldly Spiritual value of this next book, True Compassion, Merging Love into Oneness.

You generous Ones have graciously given your love, time, and ongoing support to the success of writing and publishing this book, using unique creative talents and abilities, artistry, technical skills, financial resources, and much more.

Please know that YOU are most highly appreciated! Without your support, this book would not have been born as it is into life for all of those who would surround themselves with *True Compassion, Merging Love Into Oneness.*

My heartful thanks goes out to you all, with best wishes for your continued advancement along your Spiritual journey and in your varied careers of endeavor. I continue to send, along with Ascended Master Saint Germain, highest Blessings, admiration and love.

Lah Rahn Ananda
aka Gordon Corwin II

LLantar Chris Gulve, my longtime loyal friend and Spiritual Chela, for your inspiration and support to begin this fourth published book of channeled Wisdom dedicated to enlightening Human lives in those many vitally important facets of True Compassion that you hold near and dear to your heart. Your selfless and steady encouragement throughout the creation of this book, along with contributing most capable and diligent proof reading of the manuscript, has been of value beyond description. You are acknowledged with the greatest of appreciation, with many grateful thanks from both myself as the Author and Ascended Master Saint Germain and the Realm. Love and Blessings to you. Proof reading services from: llantar@sbcglobal.net

Jossue Legaspi Aguiere, my brother in this lifetime and Soul compadre over several past-lives, I salute you for your enthusiastic willingness to support the creation of my work with Spirit. Your consciousness and Soul have rapidly grown to be an extraordinary messenger of life's lessons dynamically delivered to the Author in real time during the channeling process of this book. You continue to gift quality experiences of value in friendship, comradery and adventure, many of which were and are so very inspirational in creating this work for Humanity. You have my friendship, love and gratitude always.

Tim Yargeau, with special thanks for your kind and enthusiastic co-operation in applying your creative and very effective graphic design and photography skills, just when they were most needed! The results of your fine work, begun with the Saint Germain Chronicles Collection book project, greatly enhancing the true beauty of many graphic displays throughout the book as well. Your many image creations were also used in Saint Germain's new book '*You Me and We, Relationships that Sing to Your Soul*' which has been written and is now in the Publishing process and to be released on Amazon.
t.yargeau@gmail.com

Teri Rider, for the spectacular graphic design and image creation of the Highland Light Monogram and LOGO, banner and all!
www.teririder.com

Elaine Johnson, my old friend from Junior High School in Highland, California. After many years, we have reconnected and are able to enjoy the past and now present times together. Many thanks for your willing and gracious support in the important proof reading process of publishing this new book! Many Blessings to you.

Marius Michael-George, for the most beautiful licensed, color images of your paintings, presenting likenesses of **Ascended Masters Saint Germain and El Morya.** Artwork © Marius Michael-George
www.Mariusfineart.com

Dreamstime.com, for your print licensed permission to utilize graphic   images that add so much to illustrate text, solely inside the book in various places, with imagination and beauty.
Dreamstime.com

FCIT Florida Center for Instructional Technology, for the licensed use of your copyrighted, beautiful floral, ornate, and decorative capital letters to illustrate text, inside of the book.
licensing@fcit.us

123RF Limited, for your beautiful graphic images, print licensed for   Our use, adding so much illustrative vitality in various places, solely inside of the book.
123RF.com

Public Domain, for location of the Comte Saint Germain portrait, and the circa 1864 Charles Sindelar public domain original portrait image of Saint Germain.
The Public Domain Review

❧❧

About the Author

Gordon Corwin II, also known as Lah Rahn Ananda, translated literally as 'God Light Messenger', is a native Californian, educated at UC Berkeley, followed by service as a Commissioned US Naval Officer, and by extensive careers in the computer and real estate industries.

In 1995, Gordon clearly heard Lord Saint Germain's resounding and mysterious voice from Above, recruiting him to immediately engage with Ascended Spirit and follow his Soul's calling to reactivate his considerable past life Atlantean DNA channeling abilities, and to begin walking his Dharma to serve Humanity!

As an appointed Masters' Representative, Lah Rahn then began delivering Ascended energies through channeling of the Masters' words and visual media, which would now become his changed and conscious life path. In 1998 he founded The Light of the Soul Foundation, a qualified non-profit entity for advanced Spiritual education and Human philanthropy.

Following years of ego-cleansing by the Masters, Lah Rahn Ji has, for 25 years now, delivered clear and engaging channelings of public and private Spiritual events along with potent and enlightening mentoring of Chelas in The Light of the Soul Vortex in Southern California.

In 2007 he was highly honored to be chosen by Lord Saint Germain to be the Ascended Masters' instrument and Partner to begin, and later complete, the precise and accurate channeling of The Saint Germain Chronicles Collection, *A Journey Into Practical Spirituality 2008-2014*. In 2020 Lah Rahn again partnered with Saint Germain to write VICTORY FOR THE SOUL, *Relationships That Work, pub. 2022, and* RISING ABOVE, *A Journey Into Higher Dimensions, pub. 2022, Amazon, Gordon Corwin II,* among other unpublished channelings from Quan Yin and El Morya.

And now comes the current book, TRUE COMPASSION, Merging Love Into Oneness, pub. 2023, also available on Amazon and through worldwide book retailers.

Lah Rahn aka Gordon Corwin currently lives in Oceanside, California and is available for private channelings and group events, as well as public speaking engagements.

Contact:

GordonCorwin24@gmail.com

Lah@SaintGermainChronicles.com

DISCLAIMER

The information contained within this Book is strictly for educational purposes. This Book and the Book's elements are provided to readers committed to Spiritual education, self-discovery, self-actualization, and transformation to align individual belief systems with a common source, Our Creator and Spirit, as the guiding light to enter doorways of change, new possibilities, growth, and manifestations within reach of an extraordinary and self-examined Human lifetime. Readers are encouraged to choose, of their own free- will and volition, to accept, to follow, or to reject the guidance, ideas, philosophies, stated truths, and techniques presented herein. If you wish to apply ideas and guidance contained herein, you are taking full responsibility for your actions. This Book contains information and general advice that is intended to help the readers to be better informed about physical, mental, emotional, and Spiritual wellbeing. Always consult your doctor for your individual needs. This Book is not intended to be a substitute for the medical advice of a licensed physician. The reader should consult with their doctor in any matters relating to his/her health. This Book contains information and general advice about business pursuits. This book is not intended to be a substitute for financial or legal advice. Reader is advised to consult your licensed financial or legal professional for such matters. In no event does the author or the publisher make guarantees, express or implied, as to results or consequences arising out of or related to the reader's use or inability to use the book's contents. Both the author and Highland Light Publishers (the publisher) do not assume and hereby disclaim any liability to any party for any loss, direct, indirect, or consequential damages, accidental, unintentional, or unforeseen, pain, suffering, emotional distress, or disruption resulting from the reader's negligence, actions or non-actions, accident, or any other cause.

NOTES

NOTES

www.ingramcontent.com/pod-product-compliance
Lightning Source LLC
Chambersburg PA
CBHW040747150426
42811CB00059B/1500